Please accept this book as a Thank you for being a generous sponsor at this year's InnerVisions Gala! This book was written by one of our nurses, Rachel.

"Heart to Heart" came about when Rachel felt the urgency to share God's love to a broken world. The heart of God represents His love for us, so it is no surprise that the heart is the first organ formed during pregnancy! It is critical to provide nutrients to the developing life inside the Mother's womb. Just as Jesus is the Bread of Life for us!

A quote from Rachel. "Always remember God loves you, He created you, He has a plan for you!"

The hearts on these pages of this book were illustrations from original photos that were either taken by Rachel or given to her by family or friends. You can find these photos in the back of the book.

Heart to heart for you and me.

Heart to heart come and see!

~~~~~~~~~~~~~~~~

Give thanks to the Lord, for he is good,
His love endures forever.

PSALM 136:1

God made a perfect world...
sun, moon and sky so blue.

Mountains, oceans
and animals too.

~~~~~~~~~~~~~~~~~~~~~~~~

In the beginning God created
the heavens and the earth.

GENESIS 1:1

Heart to heart please understand,

God created YOU with a perfect plan!

~~~~~~~~~~~~~

For I know the plans I have for you, says the Lord,
plans to prosper you and not harm you,
plans to give you hope and a future.

JEREMIAH 29:11

Our heart is the first organ formed,

Inside mommy's tummy where it is safe and warm!

~~~

For you created my inmost being;
you knit me together in my mother's womb.

PSALM 139:13

He wants us to love Him
with all of our heart,

But sin entered in and
pushed us apart.

~~~~~~~~~~~~~~~~

For all have sinned and fall short of the glory of God.

ROMANS 3:23

We all need a Savior, Jesus was born on Christmas Day,

He is with us always, in every way!

~~~~~~~~~~~~~~~~~~~~~~~~~~

Today in the town of David a Savior has been born to you; he is Christ the Lord.

LUKE 2:11

God's son, Jesus,
died on the cross,

It had to be, without Him
we are lost.

~~~~~~~~~~~~~~

For God so loved the world that he gave his one
and only Son, that whoever believes in him shall not
perish but have eternal life.

JOHN 3:16

**Three days later
He came back alive,**

**He went up to Heaven,
give me a high five!**

~~~~~~~~~~~~~~~~~~~~~~~~~~~

He is not here; He has risen, just as He said...

MATTHEW 28:6

**When we say we are sorry
and turn from our sin,**

**He cleans our heart,
love and joy enter in!**

~~~~~~~~~~~~~~~~~~~~~~~~~~~~~

Repent then, and turn to God so your sins may be wiped out,
that times of refreshing may come from the Lord.

ACTS 3:19

When we read our Bibles and remember to pray,

Our hearts grow bigger every day!

~~~~~~~~~~~~~~~~~~

The fruit of the spirit is love, joy, peace, patience, kindness, goodness, faithfulness, gentleness and self control.

GALATIANS 5:22–23

God created you with
a special story,

He wants to use your life
for His glory!

~~~~~~~~~~~~~~~~~~~~~~~~~~~~~~

Whatever you do, do everything for the glory of God.

1 CORINTHIANS 10:31

In this world, Jesus is the light

Follow Him both day and night!

~~~~~~~~~~~~~~~~

I am the light of the world, whoever follows me will never walk in darkness, but will have the light of life.

JOHN 8:12

Heaven is His promise when we believe in Him with our heart,

Please help me share this message so others can be a part!

~~~~~~~~~~~~

Everyone who calls on the name of the Lord will be saved.
ROMANS 10:13

Dear Lord Jesus, I know you created me
and want me to obey you with all
of my heart. I am sorry for the times
I have disobeyed you (that's called sin).
Please forgive me.

I believe you died on the cross and rose
from the dead to save me from my sins.
I turn from my sins and invite you
to come into my heart and life.

I want to trust and obey you as
my Lord and Savior. Thank you for
your forgiveness and the promise
of Heaven for all who believe.

I love you, Jesus!

Amen

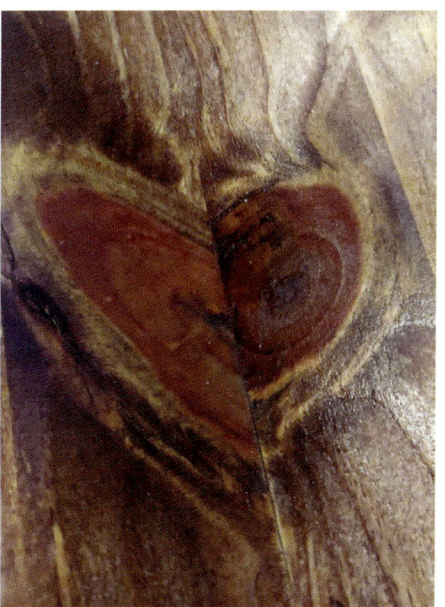

The hearts on the pages of this book
were illustrated from original photos.
As you find them throughout the years,
remember Jesus loves YOU!!

Five ways He loves you:

He created you.

PSALM 139:13

He has a plan for your life.

JEREMIAH 29:11

He sent His only son Jesus
to die on the cross for your sins.

JOHN 3:16

He forgives you.

ACTS 3:19

He is preparing a place for you in Heaven.

JOHN 14:2–4

Hearts I've Found

Date: .... Location: ....

Date: .... Location: ....

Rachel Prohaska loves being a mom to her two amazing adult children and Gigi to her grandkids. She has spent her past 20 years as a childcare provider for wonderful kids and families and enjoys working as a part-time nurse. Rachel loves Jesus, spending time with family and friends, nature, and pickleball. Heart to Heart came about these past several years after feeling the urgency of sharing God's love to a broken world. Many hearts have continued to be placed in her path, as well as the paths of kids and adults in her life. The joy of receiving pictures from kids and friends who continue to find these hearts is contagious. God loves you. He created you. He has a plan for you.

Jessica Siefert is an illustrator and designer. More of her work can be found at jessicasiefert.com.

A special thanks to my dear family, friends, and littles who have searched for hearts year after year. Thank you to my good friend's daughter, Jessica, for illustrating each page with such love!

Heart to Heart
Text and photographs copyright © 2024 by Rachel Prohaska
Illustrations copyright © 2024 by Jessica Siefert